French Laws

**An edict of the French king, prohibiting all publick exercise**

**of the pretended Reformed Religion in his kingdom**

French Laws

**An edict of the French king, prohibiting all publick exercise of the pretended Reformed Religion in his kingdom**

ISBN/EAN: 9783337274597

Printed in Europe, USA, Canada, Australia, Japan

Cover: Foto ©Suzi / pixelio.de

More available books at **www.hansebooks.com**

# AN
# EDICT
## OF THE
# French King,

Prohibiting all Publick Exercife of
the *Pretended Reformed Religion* in his Kingdom.
Wherein he Recalls, and totally An-
nuls the perpetual and irrevocable Edict of King
*Henry* the IV. his Grandfather, given at *Nantes* ;
full of moft gracious Conceffions to *Proteftants*.

To which is added,

The *French* King's Letter to the Elector of *Brandenburg*, containing feveral Paffages relating to the foregoing Edict.

As alfo, A Brief and True Account of the Perfecution
carried on againft thofe of the forefaid Religion, for to make them
Abjure and Apoftatize.

Together, With the Form of Abjuration the Revolting Proteftants are to Subfcribe and Swear to.

And a Declaration of his Electoral Highnefs of *Brandenburg*,
in Favour of thofe of the *Reformed Religion*, who fhall think fit to
fettle themfelves in any of his Dominions.

---

**Translated out of French.**

---

*The Second Edition Corrected, with Additions.*

---

Printed by G. M. *Anno Dom.* 1686.

## *An Edict of the King, Prohibiting all Publick Exercise of the* Pretended Reformed Religion *in His Kingdom.*

LEWES, by the Grace of *God*, King of *France* and of *Navarre*, to all present and to come, Greeting. King *Henry* the Great, Our Grand Father of Glorious Memory, desiring to prevent, that the Peace which he had procured for his Subjects, after the great Losses they had sustained, by the long Continuance of Civil and Foreign Wars, might not be disturbed by occasion of the *Pretended Reformed Religion*, as it had been during the Reign of the Kings, his Predecessors ; had, by his Edict given at *Nantes*, in the Month of *April*, 1598. regulated the Conduct which was to be observed, with Respect to those of the said Religion, the Places where they might publickly exercise the same, appointed extraordinary Judges, to administer Justice to them : And lastly, also, by several distinct Articles, provided for every thing, which he judged needful for the maintenance of Peace and Tranquility in his Kingdom, and to diminish the Aversion which was between those of the One and Other Religion : and this, to the end that he might be in a better condition for the taking some effectual Course (which he was resolved to do) to re-unite those again to the Church, who upon so slight Occasions had with drawn themselves from it. And forasmuch as this Intention of the King, our said Grand Father, could not be effected, by reason of his suddain and precipitated Death ; and that the Execution of the fore said Edict was Interrupted during the Minority of the late King, Our most Honoured Lord and Father, of Glorious Memory, by reason of some new Enterprizes of those of the *Pretended Reformed Religion*, whereby they gave occasion for their being deprived of several Advantages, which had been granted to them, by the afore-said Edict : notwithstanding, the King, Our said late Lord and Father, according to his wonted Clemency, granted them another Edict at *Nismes*, in the Month of *July*, 1629. by means of which the Peace and Quiet of the Kingdom being now again Re established, the said late King, being animated with the same Spirit and Zeal for

'Religion,

Religion, as the King Our said Grand-Father was, resolved to make good Use of this Tranquility, by endeavouring to put this Pious Design in Execution; but Wars abroad, coming on a few Years after, so that from the Year 1635. to the Truce which was concluded with the Princes of *Europe*, in 1684. the Kingdom having been only for some short Intervals, altogether-free from Troubles, it was not possible to do any other thing for the Advantage of Religion, save only to diminish the number of Places permitted for the Exercise of the *Pretended Reformed Religion*, as well by the Interdiction of those which were found Erected, in prejudice to the Disposal made in the said Edict, as by suppressing the Mixt Chambers of Judicature, which were composed of an equal number of *Papists* and *Protestants*; the Erecting of which was only done by Provision, and to serve the present Exigency.

Whereas therefore, at length, it hath pleased *God* to grant, that Our Subjects enjoying a perfect Peace, and We Our selves being no longer taken up with the Cares of Protecting them against Our Enemies, are now in a Condition to make good Use of the said Truce, which we have on purpose facilitated, in order to the appl·ing our selves entirely to the searching out of Means, which might successfully effect and accomplish the Design of the Kings, Our said Grand-Father and Father, and which also hath been * Our Intention ever since we came to the Crown; We see, at present, (not without a just Acknowledgment of what We owe to *God* on that Account) that Our Endeavours have attained the End We propos'd to Our selves, forasmuch as the greater and better Part of Our Subjects of the said *Pretended Reformed Religion*, have already Embraced the *Catholick*; and since, by Means thereof, the Execution of the Edict of *Nantes*, and of all other Ordinances in favour of the said *Pretended Reformed Religion*, is become useless, We judge that We can do nothing better towards the entire effacing of the Memory of those Troubles, Confusions, and Mischief, which the Progress of that false Religion hath been the cause of in Our Kingdom, and which have given Occasion to the said Edict, and to so many other Edicts and Declarations which went before it, or were made since with reference thereto, than by a Total Revocation of the said Edict of *Nantes*, and the particular Articles and Concessions granted therein, and whatsoever else hath been Enacted since, in favour of the said *Religion*.

1 We

### I.

' We make known, that We, for thefe and other Reafons Us thereto moving, and of Our certain Knowledge, full Power and Authority Royal, have by the prefent Perpetual and Irrevocable Edict, Suppreffed and Annulled, do Supprefs and Annull the Edict of the King, Our faid Grand Father, given at *Nantes,* in *April* 1598. in its whole extent, together with the particular Articles ratified the Second of *May,* next following, and Letters Patent granted thereupon; as likewife, the Edict given at *Nifmes,* in *July* 1629. declaring them null and void, as if they had never been Enacted; together with all the Conceffions granted in them, as well as other Declarations, Edicts and Arrefts, to thofe of the *Pretended Reformed Religion,* of what Nature foever they may be, which fhall all continue as if they never had been. And in purfuance hereof, We Will, and it is our Pleafure, That all the Churches of thofe of the *Pretended Reformed Religion,* fcituate in our Kingdom, Countries, Lands, and Dominions belonging to Us, be forthwith demolifhed.

### II.

We forbid our Subjects of the *Pretended Reformed Religion,* to Affemble themfelves, for time to come, in order to the Exercife of their Religion in any Place or Houfe, under what pretext foever, whether the faid Places have been granted by the Crown, or permitted by the Judges of particular places; any Arrefts of our Council, for Authorizing and Eftablifhing of the faid places for Exercife, notwithftanding.

### III.

We likewife Prohibit all Lords, of what condition foever they may be, to have any Publick Exercife in their Houfes and Fiefs, of what quality foever the faid Fiefs may be, upon penalty to all our faid Subjects, who fhall have the faid Exercifes performed in their Houfes or otherwife, of Confifcation of Body and Goods.

### IV.

We do ftrictly Charge and Command all Minifters of the faid *Pretended Reformed Religion,* who are not willing to be Converted, and to embrace the *Catholick Apoftolick* and *Roman Religion,* to depart out of our Kingdom and Countries under our Obedience, 15 days after the Publication hereof, fo as not to continue there beyond the faid term, or within the fame, to Preach, Exhort, or perform any other Minifterial Function, upon pain of being fent to the Galleys.

V. Our

### V.

Our Will and Pleasure is, That those Ministers who shall be Converted, do continue to enjoy during their Lives, and their Widows after their Decease, as long as they continue so, the same Exemptions from Payments and Quartering of Souldiers, which they did enjoy during the time of their Exercise of the Ministerial Function. Moreover, We will cause to be paid to the said Ministers, during their Lives, a Pension, which by a third part shall exceed the appointed Allowance to them as Ministers; the half of which Pension shall be continued to their Wives, after their Decease, as long as they shall continue in the State of Widow-hood.

### VI.

And in case any of the said Ministers shall be willing to become Advocates, or to take the Degree of Doctors in Law, we Will and Understand that they be dispensed with, as to the three Years of Study, which are prescribed by our Declarations, as requisite, in order to the taking of the said Degree; and that, after they have pass'd the ordinary Examinations, they be forthwith received as Doctors, paying only the Moiety of those dues, which are usually paid upon that account in every University.

### VII.

We Prohibit any particular Schools for Instructing the Children of those of the *Pretended Reformed Religion*; and in general, all other things whatsoever, which may Import a Concession, of what kind soever, in favour of the said Religion.

### VIII.

And as to the Children which shall for the future be Born of those of the said *Pretended Reformed Religion*, Our Will and Pleasure is, That henceforward they be Babtized by the Curates of our Parishes; strictly charging their respective Fathers and Mothers to take care they be sent to Church in order thereto, upon Forfeiture of 500. Livres, or more, as it shall happen. Furthermore, Our Will is, That the said Children be afterwards Educated and brought up in the *Catholick Apostolick* and *Roman Religion*, and give an express Charge to all Our Justices, to take care the same be performed accordingly.

IX. And

### IX.

And for a Mark of our Clemency towards thofe of our Subjects of the faid *Pretended Reformed Religion*, who have retired themfelves out of our Kingdom, Countries, and Territories, before the Publication of this our prefent Edict, Our Will and Meaning is, That in cafe they return thither again, within the time of four Months, from the time of the Publication hereof, they may, and it fhall be lawful for them, to Re-enter upon the Poffeffion of their Goods and Eftates, and enjoy the fame in like manner, as they might have done, in cafe they had always continued upon the place. And on the contrary, that the Goods of all thofe, who within the faid time of four Months, fhall not return into our Kingdom, Countries, or Territories under our Obedience, which they have forfaken, remain and be Confifcated in purfuance of our Declaration of the 20*th.* of *Auguft* laft.

### X.

We moft exprefly and ftrictly forbid all our Subjects of the faid *Pretended Reformed Religion*, them, their Wives or Children, to depart out of our faid Kingdom, Countries, or Territories under our Obedience, or to Tranfport thence their Goods or Effects, upon Penalty of the Gally, for Men, and of Confifcation of Body and Goods for Women.

### XI.

Our Will and Meaning is, That the Declaration made againft thofe who fhall relapfe, be Executed upon them according to their Form and Tenor.

Morever, thofe of the faid *Pretended Reformed Religion*, in the mean time, till it fhall Pleafe God to enlighten them, as well as others, may abide in the feveral refpective Cities and Places of our Kingdoms, Countries, and Territories under our Obedience, and there continue their Commerce, and enjoy their Goods and Eftates, without being any way molefted upon account of the faid *Pretended Reformed Religion*; upon condition neverthelefs, as forementioned, that they do not ufe any publick Religious Exercife, nor affemble themfelves upon the account of Prayer or Worfhip of the faid Religion, of what kind foever the fame may be, upon forfeiture above fpecified of Body and Goods.

Accordingly

Accordingly, We Will and Command our Trusty and Beloved Coun-sellors, the people holding our Courts of Aids at *Paris*, Bayliffs, Chief Juftices, Provofts, and other our Juftices and Officers to whom it appertains, and to their Lieutenants, that they caufe to be Read, Publifhed; and Regiftred, this Our prefent Edict in their Courts and Jurifdictions, even in Vacation time, and the fame keep punctually, without contrevening or fuffering the fame to be contrevened; for fuch is Our Will and Pleafure. And to the end to make it a thing firm and ftable, we have caufed Our Seal to be put to the fame. Given at *Fountainbleau*, in the Month of *October*, in the Year of Grace 1685, and of of Our Reign the XLIII.

Signed

# LEWES.

*This Signifies the*
*Lord Chancellors*  VISA.
*Perufal.*

Le Tellier.

*Sealed with the Great Seal of Green-wax,*
*upon a Red and Green ftring of Silk.*

REgiftred and Publifhed, the Kings Attorney General requiring it, in order to their being Executed according to Form and Tenor; and the Copies being Examined and Compared, fent to the feveral Courts of Juftice, Bailywicks, and Sheriffs Courts of each Diftrict, to be there Entred and Regiftred in like manner; and charge given to the Deputies of the faid Attorney General, to take care to fee the fame Executed, and put in Force; and to certifie the Court thereof. At *Paris*, in the Court of *Vacations*, the 22th. of *Octob*. 1685.

Signed

De la Baune.

Th

# A Letter of the *French* King to the Elector of *Brandenburg*, Sept. 6. 1666.

Brother,

I *Would not have difcourfed the Matter You write to Me about, on the behalf of My Subjects of the* Pretended Reformed Religion, *with any other Prince, befides Your Self : But to fhew You the particular Efteem I have for You, I fhall begin with telling You, That fome Perfons, difaffected to My Service, have fpread Seditious Pamphlets among Strangers ; as if the Acts and Edicts that were Pafs'd in favour of My faid Subjects of the* Pretended Reformed Religion, *by the Kings My Predeceffors, and Confirmed by My Self, were not kept and executed in My Dominions ; which would have been contrary to My Intentions : for I take care that they be maintained in all the Priviledges, which have been Granted them, and be as kindly us'd as My Other Subjects. To this I am Engaged both by My Royal Word, and in Acknowledgment of the Proofs they have given Me of their Loyalty, during the late Troubles, in which they took up Arms for My Service, and did vigoroufly Oppofe, and fuccefsfully Overthrow the ill Defigns which a Rebellious Party were contriving within My own Dominions, againft My Authority Royal. I pray God, &c.*

Brother, *&c.*

B

*A fhort*

*A ſhort Account of the* Violent *Proceedings,
and unheard-of Cruelties, which have been Exer-
ciſed upon thoſe of* Montauban, *and which continue to be put in Practice in other Places, againſt
thoſe of the* Reformed *Religion in* France, *for to
make them Renounce their* Religion.

ON *Saturday* the ⅛*th.* of *Auguſt*, 1685. the *Intendant* of the Upper *Guienne*, who Reſides at *Montauban*, having Summoned the Principal *Proteſtants* of the ſaid City to come before him, repreſented unto them, That they could not be ignorant, that the Abſolute Will and Plea-ſure of the King was, to Tolerate but One Religion in his Kingdom, *viz.* The *Roman Catholick Religion* ; and therefore, wiſhed them rea-dily to comply with the ſame : And in order thereto, adviſed them to Aſſemble themſelves, and conſider what Reſolution they would take. To this Propoſal ſome anſwer'd, *That there was no need of their Aſ-ſembling themſelves upon that Account ; foraſmuch as every one of them in particular, were to Try and Examine themſelves, and be always in a readineſs to give a reaſon of the Faith which was in them.*

The next Day the *Intendant* again commanded them to Meet to-gether in the Town-Houſe, which, he ordered, ſhould be left free for them from Noon, till Six of the Clock in the Evening : Where meet-ing accordingly, they Unanimouſly reſolved, as they had Lived, ſo to perſiſt till Death in their Religion : Which Reſolution of theirs, there were ſome Deputed by them to declare to the *Intendant* ; who pre-ſenting themſelves before him, he who was appointed Spokeſman, be-gan to Addreſs himſelf to the *Intendant* in theſe Words : *My Lord, We are not unacquainted, how we are menaced with the greateſt Violence.——* Hold there, ſaid the *Intendant* (interrupting him) *No Violence.* After this the *Proteſtant* continued ; *But whatever Force or Violence may be put upon us,——*Here the *Intendant* interrupting him again, ſaid, *I*
*forbid*

*forbid you to use any such Words* : Upon which Second Interruption, he contented himself to assure him in few Words, *That they were all Resolved to Live and Dye in their Religion.*

The Day after, the Battallion of *La Fere*, consisting of 16. Companies, entred the City, and were followed by many more. The *Protestants* all this while dreaming of no other Design they had against them, but that of ruining their Estates, and Impoverishing them, had already taken some Measures how to bear the said Tryal ; they had made a Common Purse, for the Relief of such who should be most burthen'd with Quartering ; and were come to a Resolution to Possess what they had, in Common : But, Alas ! how far these poor Souls were mistaken in their Accounts, and how different the Treatment they received from the *Dragoons* was, from what they had expected, I shall now Relate to you.

First therefore, in order to their Executing the Design and Project they had formed against them, they made the Souldiers take up their Quarters in one certain Place of the City ; but withal, appointed several *Corp de Guards* to cut off the Communication which One part of the City might have with the Other, and possess'd themselves of the Gates, that none might make their Escape. Things being thus ordered, the Troopers, Souldiers, and Dragoons began to Practise all manner of Hostilities, and Cruelties, where-with the Devil can Inspire the most Inhumane and Reprobate Minds : They marr'd and defac'd their Houshold-stuff, broke their Looking-Glasses, and other like Utensils and Ornaments ; they let the Wine run about their Cellars, cast abroad and spoyl'd their Corn, and other Alimentary Provisions : And as for those things which they could not break and dash to pieces, as the Furniture of Beds, Hangings, Tapistry, Linnen, Wearing Apparrel, Plate, and Things of the like Nature ; these they carried to the Market-place, where the *Jesuits* bought them of the Souldiers, and encouraged the *Roman Catholicks* to do the like. They did not stick to Sell the very Houses of such, who were most Resolute and Constant in their Profession. It is supposed, according to a Moderate Calculation, that in the time of four or five Days, the *Protestants* of that City were the poorer by a Million of Money, than they were before the entring of these Missionaries. There were Souldiers, who demanded Four hundred Crowns apiece of their Hosts for spending-Money ; and many *Protestants* were forced to pay down Ten Pistols to each Souldier, upon the same Account.

In the mean time, the outrages they committed upon their Perfons were moft deteftable and Barbarous ; I fhall only here fet down fome few, of which I have been particularly Inform'd. A certain Taylor called *Bearnois*, was bound and drag'd by the Souldiers to the *Corp de Guard*, where they Boxed and Buffetted him all Night, all which blows and Indignities he fuffered with the greateft conftancy Imaginable. The Troopers who Quartered with Monfieur *Solignac* made his Dining Room a Stable for their Horfes, tho the Furniture of it was Valued at 10000 Livres, and forc'd him to turn the Broach till his Arm was near Burnt, by their continual cafting of Wood upon the Fire. A Paffenger as he went through the faid City faw fome Souldiers beating a Poor Man even to Death, for to force him to go to Mafs, whilft the conftant Martyr to his laft Breath, cryed, *He would never do it*, and only requefted they would *Difpatch and make an end of him*. The Barons of *Cauffade* and *De la Motte*, whofe Conftancy and Piety might have Infpired Courage and Refolution to the reft of the Citizens, were fent away to *Cahors*. Monfieur *D' Alliez*, one of the prime Gentlemen of *Montauban*, being a Venerable Old Man, found fo ill Treatment at their hands, as it's thought he will fcarcely efcape with Life. Monfieur *De Garrifon*, who was one of the moft confiderable Men of that City, and an intimate Friend of the *Intendant*, went and caft himfelf at his Feet, imploring his Protection, and conjuring him to rid him of his Souldiers, that he might have no force put upon his Confcience ; adding, That in Recompence of the Favour he beg'd of him, *He would willingly give him all he had*, which was to the Value of about a Million of Livres ; but by all his Entreaties and Proffers, he could not in the leaft prevail with the *Intendant* ; who gave order, that for a Terror to the meaner fort, he fhould be worfe ufed than the reft, by dragging him along the Streets.

The Method they moft commonly made ufe of, for to make them Abjure their Religion, and which could not be the Product of any thing but Hell, was this ; Some of the moft ftrong and vigorous Souldiers, took their Hofts, or other Perfons of the Houfe, and walk'd them up and down in fome Chamber, continually tickling them and toffing them like a Ball from one to another, without giving them the leaft Intermiffion, and keeping them in this condition for three days and nights together, without Meat, Drink, or Sleep : When they were fo wearied and fainting, that they could no longer ftand upon their Legs, they laid them on a Bed, continuing as before to Tickle and Torment them ;
after

after some time, when they thought them somewhat recovered, they made them rise, and walked them up and down as before, sometimes Tickling, and other times Lashing them with Rods, to keep them from Sleeping. As soon as one Party of these Barbarous Tormenters were Tyred and wearied out, they were Relieved by others of their Companions, who coming fresh to the Work, with greater Vigour and Violence reiterated the same Course. By this Infernal Invention (which they had formerly made use of, with success, in *Bearn* and other places) many went Distracted, and others became Mopish and Stupid, and remain so.

Those who made their Escape, were fain to abandon their Estates, yea, their Wives, Children, and Aged Relations, to the Mercy of these Barbarous, and more than Savage Troops. The same Cruelties were acted at *Negrepliſſe*, a City near to *Montauban* ; where these Bloody Emiſſaries committed unparallel'd Outrages. *Iſaac Favin*, a Citizen of that Place, was hung up by his Arm-pits, and tormented a whole Night, by pinching and tearing off his Flesh with Pincers; tho by all this they were not able to shake his Constancy, in the least. The Wife of one *Renſſion*, a Joyner, being violently dragg'd by the Souldiers along the Streets, for to force her to hear Maſs, dyed of this cruel and inhumane Treatment, as soon as she reach'd the Church-Porch.

Amongst other their Devilish Inventions, this was one: They made a great Fire round about a Boy of about Ten Years of Age ; who continually, with Hands and Eyes lifted up to Heaven, cryed, *My God, help me* ; and when they saw the Lad resolved to Dye so, rather than Renounce his Religion, they snatch'd him from the Fire, when he was at the very point of being Burnt. The Cities of *Cauſſade*, *Realville*, St. *Anthonin*, and other Towns and Places in the Upper *Guienne*, met with the same Entertainment, as well as *Bergerac*, and many other Places of *Perigord*, and of the Lower *Guienne* ; which had a like share of these cruel and inhumane Uſages.

The forementioned Troops marched at last to *Caſtres*, to commit the same Insolencies and Barbarities there also: And it is not to be doubted, but that they will continue, and carry on the same course of Cruelties, where-ever they go ; if *God*, in Pity and Compaſſion to his People, do not restrain them.

It is to be feared, (for it seems but too probable) that this dreadful Persecution, in conjunction with those Artifices the *Papiſts* make use of to disguise their Religion, and to perswade *Proteſtants*, that they

shall

fhall be fuffered to Worfhip God as formerly, will make many to comply with them, or at leaft make their Mouths give their Hearts the Lye, in hopes of being by this means put into a condition to make their efcapes, and returning to that Profeffion, which their weaknefs hath made them deny.

But, Alas! this is not all; for thofe Poor Wretches, whom by thefe Devilifh ways of theirs, they have made to Blafpheme and Abjure their Religion, as if this were not enough, muft now become the Perfecutors and Tormentors of their own Wives and Children, for-to oblige and force them to Renounce alfo; for they are threatned, that if within three days time they do not make their whole Family Recant in like manner, thofe rough Apoftles (the *Dragoons*) fhall be fain to take further pains with them, in order to the perfecting of their Converfion. And who after all this can have the leaft doubt, but that thefe unhappy *Dragoons* are the very Emiffaries of Hell, whofe very laft-Efforts and Death-ftruglings thefe feem to be?

This Relation hath given a fhort view of fome of thofe Sufferings, the *Reformed* have undergone, but not of all: It is certain, that in divers places they have tryed to wear out their Patience, and overcome their Conftancy by applying Red hot Irons to the Hands and Feet of Men, and to the Breafts of Women. At *Nantes* they hung up feveral Women and Maids by their Feet, and others by their Armpits, and that Stark-Naked, thus expofing them to Publick View, which affuredly is the moft cruel and exquifite Suffering can befall that Sex; becaufe in this cafe their Shamefac'dnefs and Modefty is moft fenfibly touched, which is the moft tender part of their Soul. They have bound Mothers that gave Suck unto Pofts, and let their little Infants lye Languifhing in their fight, without being fuffered to Suckle them for feveral days, and all this while left them crying, moaning, and gafping for Life, and even Dying for Hunger and Thirft, that by this means they might Vanquifh the Conftancy of their Tender-hearted Mothers, Swearing to them they would never permit they fhould give them Suck till they promifed to Renounce their Profeffion of the Gofpel. They have taken Children of Four or Five Years of Age, and kept them from Meat and Drink for fome time, and when they have been ready to faint away and give the Ghoft, they have brought them before their Parents, and horribly Affeverated, that except they would Turn, they muft prepare themfelves to fee their Children Languifh and Dye in their prefence. Some they

have

have bound before a great Fire, and being half Roafted, have after let them go: They beat Men and Women outragioufly; they drag them along the Streets, and Torment them day and Night. The ordinary way they took, was to give them no reft; for the Souldiers do continually Relieve one another for to Drag, Beat, Torment and Tofs up and down thefe Miferable Wretches, without Intermiffion. If it happen that any by their Patience and Conftancy do ftand it out, and Triumph over all the Rage and Fury. of thofe *Dragoons*, they go to their Commander and acquaint him, they have done all they could, but yet without the defired fuccefs; who in a Barbarous and Surly Tone, anfwers them; *You muft return upon them, and do worfe than you have done; the King Commands it; either they muft Turn, or I muft Burft and Perifh in the Attempt.* Thefe are the Pleafant Flowry Paths, by which the *Papifts* allure *Proteftants* to return. to the Bofome of their Church.

But fome it may be will object; You make a great noife about a fmall matter, all *Proteftants* have not been expofed to thefe Cruelties, but only fome few obftinate Perfons: Well, I will fuppofe fo, but yet the Horror of thofe Torments Inflicted on fome, hath fo fill'd the Imagination of thefe Miferable Wretches, that the very thoughts of them hath made them comply; it is indeed a Weaknefs of which we are afhamed for their fakes, and from whence we hope God will raife them again, in his due time; yet thus much we may alledge for their excufe, that never was any Perfecution, upon pretence of Religion, carried on to that pitch, and with that Politick Malice and Cruelty that this hath been; and therefore, of all thofe which ever the Church of Chrift groan'd under, none can be compar'd with it. True indeed it is, that in former Ages it hath been common to Burn the Faithful under the Name of *Hereticks*; but how few were there expofed to that cruel kind of Death, in comparifon of thofe who efcaped the Executioners hands? But, behold here a great People at once Opprefs'd, Deftroy'd, and Ruin'd by a vaft Army of Prodigious Butchers, and few or none efcaping. Former, yea late times have given us fome Inftances of Maffacres; but thefe were only violent Tempefts, and fuddain Hurricanes, which lafted but a Night, or, at the moft, a few days, and they who fuffered in them were foon out of their pains, and the far greater number efcaped the dint of them: but how much more dreadful is the prefent condition of the *Proteftants* in *France*? And to the end we may take a true view and right

measures

meafures of it, let us confider, that nothing can be conceived more terrible, than a State of War; but what War to be compared with This? They fee a whole Army of Butcherly Canibals entring their Houfes, Battering, Breaking, Burning, and Deftroying whatever comes to hand; Swearing, Curfing, and Blafpheming like Devils; beating to excefs; offering all manner of Indignities and Violence; diverting themfelves, and ftriving to out-vie each other in inventing New Methods of Pain and Torment; not to be appeafed with Money, or good Chear; foaming and roaring like Ravenous raging Lyons; and prefenting Death, at every moment; and that which is worfe than all this, driving People to Diftraction, and fenfelefs Stupidity, by thofe Devilifh Inventions we have given you an Inftance of, in the Relation of *Montauban*.

Moreover, This Perfecution hath one Characteriftical Note more; which, without any Exaggeration, will give it the Precedence in Hiftory for Cruelty, above all thofe which the Church of *God* ever fuffered under *Nero, Maximinus,* or *Dioclefian*; which is, The fevere Prohibition of departing the Kingdom, upon pain of Confifcation of Goods, of the Gally, of the Lafh, and perpetual Imprifonment. All the Sea-Ports are kept with that Exactnefs, as if it were to hinder the Efcape of Traytors, and common Enemies: All the Prifons of Sea-Port-Towns are cramm'd with thefe miferable Fugitives, Men, Women, Boys, and Girls; who there are Condemned to the worft of Punifhments, for having had a defire to fave themfelves from this dreadful Perfecution, and deluging Calamity. This is the Thing which is unparallel'd, and of which we find no Inftance: This is thaat Superlative Excefs of Cruelty, which we fhall not find in the Lift of all the Violent and Bloody Proceedings of the Duke of *Alva*: He Maffacred, he Beheaded, he Butchered; but at leaft, he did not Prohibit thofe that could, to make their Efcape. In the laft *Hungarian* Perfecution, nothing was required of the *Proteftants*, but only that their Minifters fhould Banifh themfelves, and Abandon and Renounce the Conduct of their Flocks; and becaufe they were unwilling to obey thefe Orders, therefore it is they have groan'd under fo long, and fo terrible a Perfecution, as they have done. But this *Hungarian* Perfecution is not to be compared with that we are fpeaking of; for the Fury of that Tempeft difcharged it felf upon the Minifters only; no Armies were Imploy'd, to force the People to change their Religion, by a thoufand feveral ways of Torment; much lefs did it ever enter the Thoughts

of

of the Emperour's Councel, to shut up all the *Proteſtants* in *Hungary*, in order to the deſtroying of all thoſe who would not abjure their *Religion* ; which yet is the very condition of ſo many wretched Perſons in *France*, who beg it as the higheſt Favour at the Hands of their Merciless Enemies, to have Leave to go and beg their Bread in a Foreign Country ; being willing to leave their Goods, and all other outward Conveniencies, behind them, for to lead a poor, miſerable, languiſhing Life in any Place, where only they may be ſuffered to Dye in their Religion. And is it not from all this moſt apparent, that thoſe Monſters, who have Inſpired the King with theſe Deſigns, have refin'd the Myſtery of Perſecuting to the utmoſt, and advanc'd it to its higheſt Pitch of Perfection ?

*O Great God! who from thy Heavenly Throne, do'ſt behold all the Outrages done to thy People, haſte Thee to help us! Great God, whoſe Compaſſions are Infinite, ſuffer thy Self to be touched with our extream Deſolation! If Men be Inſenſible of the Calamities we ſuffer, if they be deaf to our Cries, not regarding our Groans and Supplications ; yet let thy Bowels, O* Lord, *be moved, and affect Thee in our behalf. Glorious God, for whoſe Names ſake we ſuffer all theſe things, who knoweſt our Innocence and Weakneſs, as well as the Fury and Rage of our Adverſaries, the ſmall Support and Help we find in the World ; Behold, we periſh, if thy Pity doth not rouze Thee up for our Relief. It is Thou art our Rock, our God, our Father, our Deliverer: We do not place our Confidence in any, but Thee alone : Let us not be confounded, becauſe we put our Truſt in Thee. Haſte Thee to our Help ; make no long tarrying. O* Lord, *our* God, *and our Redeemer!*

---

## A Letter ſent from Bourdeaux, giving an Account of the Perſecution of thoſe of the Proteſtant Religion in France.

*SIR,*

WHat you have heard concerning the Perſecution of thoſe that are of our *Religion*, in the Land of *Bearne, Guienne,* and *Perigord*, is but too true ; and I can aſſure you, that they who have given you that Account, have been ſo far from amplifying the Matter,

that

that they have only acquainted you with some few particulars; yet am I not much surprized at the difficulty you find to perswade your self, that the things of which your Friends Inform you, are true: In cases of this Nature, so amazingly unexpected, we are apt often to distrust our own Eyes; and I profess to you, that though all places round about us Echo the Report of our Ruine and Destruction, yet I can scarcely perswade my self it is so indeed, because I cannot comprehend it. It is no matter of surprize, or amazement, to see the Church of *Christ* afflicted upon Earth, forasmuch as she is a stranger here, as well as her Captain, Lord and Husband, the Holy and Everblessed *Jesus* was;-and must, like Him, by the same way of Cross and Suffering, return to her own Country, which is above. It is no matter of Astonishment, to find her from time to time suffering the worst of usage, and most cruel Persecutions; all Ages have seen her exposed to such Tryals as these, which are so necessary for the Testing of her Faith, and so fit a matter of her Future Glory. Neither is it any great wonder, if, amidst these sore Tryals, vast numbers of those who made Profession of the Gospel, do now Renounce and forsake it: We know that all have not Faith; and it is more than probable, that they who do not follow *Christ*, but because they Thrive by it, and for the Loaves, will cease to be of his Retinue, when he is about to oblige them to bear his Cross, and deny themselves. But that which seems Inconceivable to me, is, that our Enemies should pitch upon such strange ways and methods to destroy us, as they have done, and that, in so doing, they should meet with a success so prodigious and doleful. I shall as briefly as I can endeavour to give you an account of so much as I have understood of it.

All those thundring Declarations, and destructive Arrests, which continually were Sued for, and obtain'd against us, and which were Executed with the Extremity of Rigour, were scarce able to move any one of us. The forbidding of our Publick Exercises, the demolishing of our Churches, and the severe Injunction that not so much as Two or Three of us should dare to Assemble, in order to any thing of Divine Worship, had no other effect upon the far greater part of us, than to Inflame our Zeal, instead of abating it; obliging us to Pray to *God* with greater Fervor, and Devotion in our Closets, and to Meditate of his Word with greater Application and Attention. And neither the great wants, to which we were reduced by being depriv'd of our Offices and Imploys, and all other means of Living, and by those

those insupportable charges with which they strove to over-whelm us, as well by Taxes, as the Quartering of Souldiers (both which were as heavy as could be laid upon us) nor the continual trouble we were put to by Criminal or other matters of Law, which at the Suit of one or other were still laid to our charge, tho upon the most frivolous and unjust pretences imaginable ; I say, all these were not able to wear out our Patience, which was hardned against all Calamities : insomuch as the design of forcing us to abandon the Truth of the Gospel, would Infallibly have been Ship-wrack'd, if no other means had been taken in hand for this purpose. But, Alas! our Enemies were too Ingenious, to be bauk'd so; and had taken our Ruine too much to Heart, not to study for means effectual and proper to bring about their desires: They call'd to mind what Prodigious success a new kind of Persecution had had of late Years in *Poctou*, *Aunix*, and *Xaintonge*, which the *Intendants* of those places had bethought themselves of ; and they made no difficulty to have Recourse to the same, as to a means Infallible, and not to be doubted of.

I must tell you, *Sir*, That we had not the least thought that ever such violent Methods as these, would have been pitched upon, as the means of our Conversion: We were always of Opinion, that none but *Dennnienx's*, and *Marillacs*, could be fit Instruments for such like Enterprizes ; neither could we ever have Imagin'd, that Generals of Armies, who account it a Shame and Reproach to Attack and take some paultry Town or Village, should ever debase themselves to Besiege Old Men, Women, and Children in their own Houses ; or that ever Souldiers, who think themselves ennobled by their Swords, should degrade themselves so far, as to take up the Trade of Butchers and Hangmen, by tormenting poor Innocents, and inflicting all sorts of Punishments upon them.

Moreover, we were the less in expectation of any such thing, because at the self-same time they Treated us in this manner, they would needs perswade us, *That the King's Councel had disapproved the Design*: And indeed, it seem'd very probable to us, that all Reasons, whether taken from Humanity, Piety, or Interest, would have made them disavow and condemn a Project so Inhumane and Barbarous : Yet now, by Experience, we find it but too true, that our Enemies are so far from rejecting the said Design, that they carry it on with an unparallel'd Zeal and Application, without giving themselves any further trouble to effectuate their Desires, than that of doing these two things:

The

The First of which was, to Lull us asleep, and to take away from us all matter of Suspition of the mischief they were hatching against us; which they did by permitting some of our Publick Exercises of Religion, by giving way to our Building of some Churches, by settling Ministers in divers places to Baptize our Children, and by publishing several Arrests and Declarations, which did intimate to us, that we had reason to hope we should yet Subsist for some Years: Such was that Declaration, by which all Ministers were ordered to change their Churches every three years.

The Other was, to secure all the Sea-Ports of the Kingdom, so as none might make their escape, which was done by renewing the Antient Prohibitions of departing the Kingdom without leave, but with the addition of far more severe Penalties.

After these precautions thus taken, they thought themselves no longer oblig'd to keep any measures, but immediately lift up the hand, to give the last blow for our Ruine. The *Intendants* had order to represent to us, *That the King was resolved to suffer no other Religion in his Kingdom besides his own, and to Command us all in his Name, readily to Embrace the same, without allowing us any longer respite to consider what we had to do, than a few days, nay hours;* threatning us, *That if we continued obstinate, they would force us to it by the extremity of Rigour; and presently Executing these their Menaces, by filling our Houses with Souldiers, to whom we were to be left for a Prey; and who, not content with entirely Ruining of us, should besides exercise upon our Persons all the Violence and Cruelty they could possibly devise:* And all this to overcome our Constancy and Perseverance.

Four Months are now past and gone, since they began to make use of this strange and horrible way of Converting People, worthy of, and well becoming its Inventors. The Country of *Bearne* was first set upon, as being one of the most considerable Out-parts of the Kingdom, to the end that this mischievous enterprize gaining strength in its passage, might soon after over-whelm, and as it were deluge all the other Provinces in the same Sea of the uttermost calamity. Monsieur *Foucaut* the Intendant, went himself in Person to all the places where we were in any numbers, and commanded all the Inhabitants that were of the Protestant Religion, under the Penalty of great amercements, to Assemble themselves in those places he appointed to them; where, being accordingly met together, he charged them in the Kings Name to change their Religion, allowing them only a day,

or

or two to dispose themselves for it : He told them, *That great numbers of Souldiers were at hand, to compel those that should refuse to yield a ready Obedience* ; and this threatning of his being immediately followed by the Effect, as Lightning is by Thunder, he fill'd the Houses of all those who abode constant in their resolution to Live and Dye Faithful to their Lord and Master, *Jesus Christ*, with Souldiers ; and Commands those Insolent Troops ( flesh'd with Blood and Slaughter ) to give them the worst Treatment they could possibly devise.

I shall not undertake, *Sir*, to give you a particular Account of those Excesses, and Outrages, these enraged Brutals committed in Executing the Orders they were charged with ; The Relation would prove too tedious and doleful: It shall suffice me to tell you, That they did not forget any thing that was Inhumane, Barbarous, or Cruel, without having regard to any Condition Sex or Age ; they pull'd down and demolished their Houses ; they spoil'd, dash'd to pieces, and burnt their best Moveables and Houshold-stuff ; they bruised and beat to Death Venerable Old Men ; they dragg'd Honourable Matrons to Mass, without the least pitty or respect ; they bound and Fetter'd Innocent Persons, as if they had been the most Infamous and Profligate Villains ; they hung them up by their Feet, till they saw them ready to give up the Ghost ; they took Red-hot Fire-shovels, and held them close to their bare Heads, and actually apply'd them to other parts of their Bodies ; they Immur'd them within four Walls, where they let them Perish for Hunger and Thirst : And the Constancy wherewith they suffer'd all these Torments, having had no other effect, but that of augmenting the Rage of these Furies, they never ceased Inventing new ways of Pain and Torture, till their Inhumanity at length had got the Victory, and Triumphed over the Patience and Faith of these Miserable Wretches. Insomuch, that of all those many numerous Assemblies, we had in that Province, as that of *Pau, d'Arthes, de Novarre, &c.* there are scarcely left a small number, who either continue constant in despite of all these Cruelties, or else have made their escape into *Spain, Holland, England*, or elsewhere, leaving their Goods and Families for a Prey to these Merciless and Cruel Men.

Success having thus far answered their Expectation, they resolved to lose no time, but vigorously Prosecuting their work, they immediately turned their Thoughts and Arms towards *Montauban* ; where the *Intendant* having Summoned the Citizens to appear before him, bespeaks

befpeaks them much of the fame Language, as was ufed to thofe of
Bearne; whereunto they having returned about the fame Anfwer, he
orders 4000. Men to enter the City, and makes them take up their
Quarters, as at Bearne, only in the Houfes of Protestants; with ex-
pref Command to Treat them in like manner, as they had done thofe
of Bearne: And thefe Inhumane Wretches were fo diligent and active
in Executing thefe pittilefs Orders, that of 12, or 15000. Souls, of which
that Church did confift, not above 20, or 30. Families are efcaped;
who, in a doleful and forlorn Condition, wander up and down the
Woods, and hide themfelves in Thickets. The Ruine of this Important
Place, drew after it the Defolation of all the Churches about it;
which were all Enveloped in the fame common Calamity, as thofe of
Realmont, Bourniquel, Negrepliffe, &c.

Yet was not the Condition of the Churches in the Upper Guienne
more fad and calamitous, than that of thofe of the Lower Guienne,
and of Perigord; which this horrible Deluge hath likewife overwhelm'd.
Monfieur Boufler's, and the Intendant, having fhared the Country between them; Monfieur de Boufler taking for his Part Agenois, Tonnein,
Clerac, with the adjoyning Places; and the Intendant having taken
upon him to reduce Fleis, Montravel, Genffac, Cartillon, Contras, Li-
bourne, &c. The Troops which they commanded, in the mean time,
carrying Defolation to all the Places they paffed through, filling them
with Mourning and Defpair, and fcattering Terror and Amazement
amongft all thofe to whom they approached.

There were at the fame time 17. Companies at Saint Foy, 15. at Ne-
rac, and as many in proportion in all other Parts: So that, all Places
being fill'd with thefe Troops, accuftom'd to Licentioufnefs and Pil-
lage, there is not any one of the faid Places, where they have not left
moft dreadful Marks of their Rage and Cruelty; having at laft, by
means of their exquifite Tortures, made all thofe of our Religion fub-
mit themfelves to the Communion of Rome.

But forafmuch as Bergerac was moft fignally Famous for the long
Tryals it had moft Glorioufly endured, and that our Enemies were
very fenfible of what Advantage it would be, to the carrying on of their
Defign, to make themfelves Mafters there alfo, at any price wharfo-
ever; they accordingly fail'd not to attempt the fame with more Refolution and Obftinacy, than any of the forementioned Places.

This little Town had already, for Three Years together, with ad-
mirable Patience and Conftancy, endured a Thoufand ill Treatments,
and

and Exactions from Souldiers, who had pick'd them to the very Bones; for besides that, it was almost a continual passage for Souldiers; there were no less than 18. Troops of Horse had their Winter-Quarters there; who yet in all that time had only gain'd Three Converts, and they such too as were maintain'd by the Alms of the Church.

But to return: The design being form'd to reduce this City, two Troops of Horse are immediately ordered thither, to observe the Inhabitants, and soon after 32 Companies of Foot enter the Town: Monsieur *Boufflers* and the Intendant of the Province, with the Bishops of *Agen* and *Perigueux*, and some other Persons of Quality, render themselves there at the same time, and send for 200. of the chiefest Citizens to appear before them; telling them, *That the Kings Express Will and Pleasure was, they should all go to Mass; and that in case of Disobedience, they had order to compel them to it:* To which the Citizens Unanimously answered, *That their Estates were at the dispose of his Majesty, but that God alone was Lord of their Consciences; and that they were resolved to suffer to the utmost, rather than do any thing contrary to the motions of it.* Whereupon they were told, *That if they were so resolved, they had nought else to do but to prepare themselves to receive the Punishment their Obstinacy and Disobedience did deserve;* and immediately 32. Companies more, of Infantry and Cavalry, enter the City (which, together with the 34 Companies beforementioned, were all Quartered with *Protestants*) with Express Command not to spare any thing they had, and to exercise all manner of Violence upon the Persons of those that entertain'd them, until they should have extorted a Promise from them, to do whatsoever was Commanded them.

These Orders then being thus Executed, according to the desires of those who had given them, and these miserable Victims of a Barbarous Military Fury, being reduc'd to the most deplorable and desolate condition; they are again sent for to the Town-house, and once more pressed to change their Religion; and they answering with Tears in their Eyes, and with all the Respect, Humility, and Submission imaginable, *That the matter required of them, was the only thing they could not do,* the extreamest Rigour and Severity is denounc'd against them; and they presently made good their Words, by sending 34. more Companies into the City, which made up the full number of an hundred; who encouraging themselves from their numbers, and flying like enraged Wolves upon these Innocent Sheep, did rend and worry them in such a manner, as the sole Relation cannot but strike with Horror

and

and Amazement. Whole Companies were ordered to Quarter with one Citizen; and Perſons whoſe whole Eſtate did not amount to 10000. Livres, were taxed at the rate of 150. Livres a day : When their Money is gone, they ſell their Houſhold-ſtuff, and ſell that for two pence, which hath coſt 60. Livres; they bind and fetter Father, Mother, Wife and Children : Four Souldiers continually ſtand at the door, to hinder any from coming-in to ſuccour or comfort them : they keep them in this condition, two, three, four, five, and ſix days, without either Meat, Drink, or Sleep : On one hand the Child cries, with the Languiſhing accent of one ready to Dye, *Ah my Father! Ah my Mother! What ſhall I do? I muſt Dye, I can endure no longer*: The Wife on the other hand cries, *Alas! my Heart fails me, I Faint, I Dye!* Whilſt their cruel Tormentors are ſo far from being touch'd with Compaſſion, that from thence they take occaſion to preſs them afreſh; and to renew their Torments, frighting them with their Helliſh Menaces, accompanied with moſt execrable Oaths and Curſes; crying, *Dog, Bougre, What, wilt not thou be Converted? Wilt not thou be Obedient?* *Dog, Bougre, Thou muſt be Converted, we are ſent on purpoſe to Convert thee*: And the Clergy, who are witneſſes of all theſe Cruelties, ( with which they feaſt their Eyes ) and of all their Infamous and abominable words; (which ought to cover them with Horror and Confuſion ) make only a matter of Sport and Laughter of it.

Thus theſe miſerable Wretches, being neither ſuffered to Live nor to Dye, ( for when they ſee them fainting away, they force them to take ſo much as to keep Body and Soul together) and ſeeing no other way for them to be delivered out of this Hell, in which they are continually Tormented, are fain at laſt to ſtoop under the unſupportable Burthen of theſe extremities : So that, excepting only a few who ſaved themſelves by a timely Flight, preferring their Religion before all Temporal Poſſeſſions, all the reſt have been conſtrained to go to Maſs.

Neither is the Country any more exempt from theſe Calamities, than Towns and Cities ; nor thoſe of the Nobility and Gentry, than Citizens. They ſend whole Companies of Souldiers into Gentlemens Houſes, who Treat them in the moſt outragious and violent manner conceivable, inſomuch that not a Soul can hope to eſcape, except it may be ſome few, who like the Believers of old, wander in Deſarts, and lodge in Dens and Caves of the Earth.

Further-

Furthermore, I can assure you, that never was any greater Conster-hation, than that which we are in here at present; the Army, we hear, is come very near us, and the *Intendant* is just now Arrived in this City; the greater part of the most considerable Merchants are either already gone, or casting about how best to make their escape, abandoning their Houses and Estates to their Enemies; and there are not wanting some Cowardly Spirits, who, to avoid the mischief they are preparing for us, have already promised to do whatsoever is required of them. In a word, nothing is seen or heard in these parts but Consternation, Weeping and Lamentation; there being scarce a Person of our Religion, who hath not his Heart pierced with the bitterest Sorrows, and whose Countenance hath not the Lively Picture of Death Imprinted on it: and surely, if our Enemies Triumph in all this, their Triumph cannot likely be of any long continuance.

I confess, I cannot perswade my self to entertain so good an opinion of them, as to think that ever they will be ashamed of these their doings, so Diametrically opposite to the Spirit of the Gospel; for I know the Gospel, in their accounts, passeth for a Fable: but this I dare averr, that this Method of theirs will Infallibly lay waste the Kingdome, which, according to all appearance, is never like to recover of it; and so in time, they themselves will be made as sensible of these miseries, as others now are. Commerce is already in a manner wholly extinct, and there will need little less than a Miracle to recover it to its former State. What *Protestant* Merchants will hence-forward be willing to engage themselves in Trade, either with Persons without Faith; and who have so cowardly betray'd their Religion and Conscience, or with the Outragious and Barbarous Persecuters of the Religion, which they profess? and who by these courses declare openly and frankly, that it is their Principle, not to think themselves oblig'd to keep their word with Hereticks? And who are those, of what Religion soever, that will Negotiate with a State exhausted by Taxes and Subsidies, by Persecutions, by Barrenness and Dearth of several years continuance; full of a despairing People, and which Infallibly will e're long be full of those that are proscrib'd, and be bathing in its own Blood.

And these miserable Wretches, who have been deceived by those who have told them, That it would never be impos'd upon them to abjure their Religion, and who are stupified by the extremity of their Sufferings, and the terror of their bloody and cruel Enemies, are wrapt

D                                                                up up in so deep an Astonishment, as doth not permit them to be fully sensible of their Fall : But as soon as they shall recover themselves, and remember, that they could not Embrace the Communion of *Rome*, without absolutely Renouncing the Holy *Religion* they Professed ; and when they shall make a full Reflection upon the unhappy Change they have been forced to make; then their Consciences being awakened, and continually reproaching their Faint-heartedness, will rend them with Sorrow and Remorse, and inflict Torments upon them, equal to those the Damned endure in Hell ; and will make them endeavour to be delivered from this Anguish, and to find Rest in the constant Profession of that Truth, which they have unhappily betray'd.

And on the other side ; Their Enemies will be loath to take the Lye at this time of the Day ; and therefore will endeavour, through fear of Punishments, to oblige them to stay in that Abyss of Horror, into which they have precipitated them : But because all the Sufferings they can possibly threaten them with, will be no ways considerable, when compared with those Tortures their Consciences have already Inflicted upon them, and where-with they threaten them in case of a Relapse, they will be constrained to drag them to the Place of Execution, or else seek to rid themselves of them all at once, by a general Massacre, which many good Souls have so long desired.

I hope, *Sir*, You will not be wanting in your most earnest Prayers to beg of *God*, that He would be pleased to take pity of these miserable Wretches ; and make the Heart of our Soveraign to relent towards us; That He would Convert those, who in their Blindness think they do Him Service, by putting us to Death; That He would cause his Voice to be heard by them from Heaven, as to St. *Paul* ; *Saul, Saul, Why Persecutest thou me ?* And make the rest the Examples of his Exemplary Justice : Finally, That He would grant, That all those who have denied Him, being touched with a True Repentance, may, with St. *Peter, Go out, and Weep bitterly.* I am,

*S I R,*

*Yours, &c.*

*An*

## An Extract of a Letter, containing some more Instances of the Cruel and Barbarous Usage of the Protestants in France.

BUt this, *Sir*, is not the thing which troubles me most, at this time; there's another cause of my Grief, which is but too just, and even pierceth my Heart with Sorrow; and that is, The Cruel Persecution, which the Poor *Protestants* of *France* do suffer, amongst whom I have so many near and dear Relations: The Torments they are put to, are almost Incredible; and the Heavenly Courage, wherewith some of them are strengthned by their Great Captain and Leader, to undergo them, is no less amazing and wonderful: I shall give for Instance one or two of these Champions, that by them you may judge of the rest.

A Young Woman was brought before the Council, in order to oblige her to abjure the Truth of the Gospel; which she boldly and manfully refusing, was commanded back again to Prison; where they shaved her Head, and sing'd off the Hair of her Privities; and having stript her Stark-Naked, in this manner led her through the Streets of the City; where many a blow was given her, and Stones flung at her. After this, they set her up to the Neck in a Tub full of Water; where after she had been for a while, they took her out, and put upon her a Shift dipt in Wine, which as it dry'd, and stuck to her Sore and Bruised Body, they snatch'd off again; and then had another ready, dipt in Wine, to clap upon her: This they repeated six several times; and when by this inhumane usage, her Body was become very Raw and Tender, they demanded of her, *Whether she did not now find her self disposed to Embrace the Catholick Faith?* for so they are pleased to term their Religion: But she, being strengthned by the Spirit and Love of Him, for whose Names sake she suffered all these Extremities, undauntedly answer'd; *That she had before declared her Resolution to them, which she would never alter; and that, though they had her Body in their Power, she was resolved not to yield her Soul to them; but keep it pure and undefiled for her Heavenly Lover; as knowing, that a little while would put an end to all her Sufferings, and give a*

D 2

*Beginning to her Enjoyment of Everlasting Bliss:* Which Words of hers, adding Fuel of their Rage, who now despaired of making her a Convert, they took and fastned her by her Feet, to something that served the turn of a Gibbet, and there let her hang in that Ignominious Posture, with her Head downwards, till she expired.

The other Person I would instance in, and whom I pity the more, because (for ought I know) he may yet survive, and still continue under the Tormentor's Hands, is an Old Man; who having, for a great while, been kept close Prisoner (upon the same Account as the former) in a deep Dungeon, where his Companions were Darkness and Horror, and filthy Creeping Things, was brought before his Judges, with Vermin and Snails crawling upon his Mouldred Garment; who seeing him in that Loathsom Condition, said to him: *How now Old Man, does not your Heart begin to Relent? and are not you willing to Abjure your Heresie?* To which he answer'd: *As for Heresie, I profess none; but if by that Word you mean my Religion, you may assure your selves, that as I have thus long Lived, so, I hope, and am resolved by the Grace of God, to Dye in it:* With which Answer they being little pleased, but furiously Incensed, bespoke him in a rougher Tone: *Do'st thou not see, that the Worms are about to devour thee? Well, since thou art so resolved, we will send thee back again, to the loathsom Place from whence thou camest, that they may make an end of thee, and consume thy obdurate Heart:* To which he reply'd, with the Words of the Holy Patient *Job; Novi postquam vermes confoderint (Corpus) istud, in carne mea me visurum esse Deum. I know that after Worms have eaten this Body, that in my Flesh I shall see God.* And having so said, he was sent back to his loathsom dark Abode; where if he be still, I pray *God* to give him Patience and Strength to hold out to the End, that so he may obtain the Crown of Life.

I should be too tedious, in giving you all the Particulars of their Cruelty, and of the Sufferings of the *Protestants;* yet I cannot well forbear acquainting you with what lately I am most credibly inform'd of; which take as follows: Some *Dragoons,* who were Quartered with a Person, who they could by no means oblige to Renounce his Religion; upon a time, when they had well fill'd themselves with Wine, and broke their Glasses at every Health they drank; and so fill'd the Floor, where they were, with the Fragments; and by often walking over, and treading upon them, reduced them to lesser Pieces and Fractions: And being now in a merry Humour, they must needs

go

go to Dance ; and told their Host, That he must be One of the Company ; but withal, that he must first pull off his Stockings and Shoes, that he might move the more nimbly : In a word, they forc'd him to Dance with them bare-footed, upon the sharp Points of Glass ; which when they had continued so long as they were able to keep him on his Legs, they laid him down on a Bed ; and a while after stript him stark naked, and rolled his Body from one end of the Room to the other, upon the sharp Glass, as beforementioned ; which having done, till his Skin was stuck full of the said little Fragments, they returned him again to his Bed, and sent for a Chyrurgeon, to take out all the said Pieces of Glass out of his Body ; which, you may easily conceive, could not be done without frequent Incisions, and horrible and most extream Pain. Another Person being likewise troubled with the unwelcome Company of these *Dragoons*, and having suffered extreamly at their Hands, without the expected Success of his Conversion ; one of them on a time looking earnestly upon him, told him, *That he disfigured himself, with letting his Beard grow so long :* But he answering, *That they were the cause of it, who would not let him stir out of door, for to go to the Barber :* The *Dragoon* reply'd *I can do that for you as well as the Barber ;* and with that told him, *He must needs try his Skill upon him :* And so fell to work ; but instead of shaving him, flea'd all the Skin off his Face. One of his Companions coming-in at the Cry of this poor Sufferer, and seeing what he had done, seemingly blam'd him for it, and said, *He was a Bungler ;* and then to his Host, *Come, your Hair wants Cutting too ; and you shall see, I will do it much better than he hath shav'd you :* And thereupon begins, in a most cruel manner, to pluck the Hair, Skin, and all, off his Head, and flea'd That as the other had done his Chin. Thus making a Sport and Merriment of the extream Suffering of these miserable Wretches.

By these Inhumane, and more than Barbarous means it is, that they endeavour to overcome the most resolved Patience, and to drive People to Despair and Faint-heartedness, by their Devilish Inventions. They refuse to give them Death, which they desire ; and only keep them alive to torment them, so long till they have vanquish'd their Perseverance ; for the Names of *Martyrs,* and *Rebels,* are equally odious to their Enemies ; who tell them, *That the King will have Obedient Subjects, but neither Martyrs nor Rebels ; and that they have received Orders to Convert them, but not to Kill them.*

*Sir,* I beg your Pardon, for having so long Entertain'd you with these more than Tragical Passages; and that you would not be wanting to recommend the Condition of these Poor, Destitute, Afflicted, and Tortured Persons, to the Bowels of Compassion of our Heavenly Father, that He would be pleased not to suffer them to be Tempted above what he shall give them Grace to bear: Which is the Hearty Prayer of,

Your Faithful Friend,

*T. G.*

---

*Since the First Publishing of This, some further Particulars (representing the Horror of this Persecution) are come to hand; which take as follow:*

THey have put Persons into Monasteries, in little narrow holes, where thy could not stretch their Bodies at length; there Feeding them with Bread and Water, and Whipping them every day, till they did Recant: They plunged others into Wells, and there kept them till they promised to do what was desired of them: They stript some Naked, and stuck their Bodies full of Pins: They tyed Fathers and Husbands to the Bed-Posts, forcing their Wives and Daughters before their Eyes: In some Places, the Ravishing of Women was openly and generally permitted: They pluck'd off the Nails and Toes of others: They Burnt their Feet, and blew up Men and Women with Bellows, till they were ready to Burst. In a word, They exercised all manner of Cruelties they could invent; and in so doing, spared neither Sex, Age nor Quality.

*The*

*The Profession of the Catholick, Apostolick, and Ro-
man Faith, which the Revolting Protestants in
France are to Subscribe and Swear to.*

IN *the Name of the Father, Son, and Holy Ghost,* Amen. *I Believe and
Confess with a firm Faith, all and every thing and things contained in
the Creed, which is used by the Holy Church of* Rome, viz. *I Receive
and Embrace most sincerely the Apostolick and Ecclesiastical Traditions,
and other Observances of the said Church. In like manner, I receive the
Scriptures, but in the same Sence as the said Mother Church hath, and
doth now understand and Expound the same ; for whom and to whom it
only doth belong to judge of the Interpretation of the Sacred Scriptures :
And I will never take them, nor understand them otherwise, than according to the unanimous Consent of the Fathers.*

*I profess, That there be truly and properly Seven Sacraments of the
New Law, instituted by our Lord* Jesus Christ, *and necessary for the Sal-
vation of Mankind, altho' not equally needful for every one,* viz. Baptism,
Confirmation, *the* Eucharist, Penance, Extream Unction, Orders and
Marriage; *and that they do confer Grace ; and that* Baptism and Orders
*may not be reiterated, without Sacriledge : I receive and admit also the
Ceremonies received and approved by the Catholick Church, in the
solemn Administration of the forementioned Sacraments.*

*I receive and embrace all and every thing, and things, which have been
determined concerning Original Sin and Justification by the Holy Council of* Trent.

*I likewise profess, that in the* Mass *there is offered up to* God, *a true,
proper, and propitiatory Sacrifice for the Living and Dead ; and that in
the Holy Sacrament of the* Eucharist, *there is* truly, really, and Substan-
tially, the Body and Blood, together with the Soul and Divinity of the
Lord Jesus Christ; *and that in it there is made a change of the whole
Substance of the Bread into his Body, and of the whole Substance of the Wine
into his Blood ; which change the Catholick Church calls* Transubstantia-
tion. *I confess also, That under one only of these two Elements, whole*
Christ, *and the true Sacrament is received.*

*I constantly believe and affirm, that there is a Purgatory; and that the
Souls there detained, are relieved by the Suffrages of the Faithful.*

*In like manner, I believe that the Saints Reigning in Glory with* Jesus
Christ;

Chriſt, are to be Worſhipped and Invocated by us, and that they offer up Prayers to God for us, and that their Reliques ought to be honoured.

Moreover, I do moſt ſtedfaſtly avow, that the Images of Jeſus Chriſt, of the Bleſſed Virgin, the Mother of God, and of other Saints, ought to be kept and retained, and that due Honour and Veneration muſt be yielded unto them.

Alſo I do affirm, that the power of Indulgence was left to the Church by Chriſt Jeſus, and that the uſe thereof is very beneficial to Chriſtians.

I do acknowledge the holy Catholick, Apoſtolick, and Roman Church, to be the Mother and Miſtreſs of all other Churches; and I Profeſs and Swear true Obedience to the Pope of Rome, Succeſſor of the Bleſſed St. Peter, Prince of the Apoſtles, and Vicar of Jeſus Chriſt.

In like manner, I own and profeſs, without doubting, all other things left defined and declared by the Holy Canons and General Councils, eſpecialy by the moſt Holy Council of Trent; and withal, I do condemn, rejeʄ, and hold for accurſed, all things that are contrary thereto; and all thoſe Hereſies which have been condemned, rejeʄed, and accurſed by the Church.

And then Swearing upon the Book of the Goſpel, the Party Recanting muſt ſay: I Promiſe, Vow, and Swear, and moſt conſtantly Profeſs, by Gods Aſſiſtance, to keep entirely and inviolably, unto Death, this ſelf-ſame Catholick and Apoſtolick Faith, out of which no Perſon can be Saved; and this I do moſt truly and willingly profeſs, and that I will to the utmoſt of my Power endeavour that it may be maintain'd and upheld as far as any ways belong to my Charge; ſo help me God, and the Holy Virgin.

## The Certificate which the Party Recanting is to leave with the Prieſt, when he makes his Abjuration.

I N. N. of the Pariſh of N. do Certifie all whom it may Concern, That having acknowledged the Falſeneſs of the Pretended Reformed, and the Truth of the Catholick Religion, of my own Free will, without any Compulſion, I have accordingly made Profeſſion of the ſaid Catholick Roman Religion in the Church of N. in the hands of N. N. In Teſtimony of the Truth whereof, I have Signed this Act in the preſence of the Witneſſes whoſe Names are under Written, this —— day of the Month of the —— Year of the Reign of our Soveraign Lord the King, and of our Redemption ——

*A*

# A Declaration of the Elector of Brandenburg, in Favour of the French Protestants, who shall Settle themselves in any of His Dominions.

We *Frederick William*, by the Grace of *God*, Marquess of *Brandenburg*, Arch-Chamberlain, and Prince Elector of the *Holy Empire* ; Duke of *Prussia*, *Magdeburg*, *Juilliers*, *Cleves*, *Bergen*, *Stettin*, *Pomerania* ; of the *Cassubes*, *Vandals*, and *Silesia* ; of *Crosne*, and *Jagerndorff* ; Burg-grave of *Noremberg* ; Prince of *Halberstadt*, *Minde*, and *Camin* ; Earl of *Hohenzollern*, of the *Mark* and *Ravensberg* ; Lord of *Ravenstein*, *Lawneburg*, and *Butow*, do declare and make known to all to whom these Presents shall come :

THat whereas the Perfecutions and Rigorous Proceedings which have been carried on for some time in *France*, against those of the *Reformed Religion*, have forced many Families to leave that Kingdom, and to seek for a Settlement elsewhere, in strange and Foreign Countries ; We have been willing, being touched with that just Compassion, We are bound to have for those who suffer for the Gospel, and the Purity of that Faith We profess, together with them, by this present Declaration, Signed with Our own Hand, to offer, to the said *Protestants*, a sure and free Retreat in all the Countries and Provinces under Our Dominion ; and withal, to declare the several Rights, Immunities, and Priviledges, which We are willing they shall enjoy there, in order to the Relieving and easing them, in some measure, of the burthen of those Calamities, wherewith it hath pleased the Divine Providence to afflict so considerable a Part of his Church.

To

### I.

To the end, that all those who shall resolve to Settle themselves in any of our Dominions, may with the more Ease and Convenience Transport themselves thither, We have given Order to our Envoy extraordinary with the States-General of the *United Provinces*, *Sieur Diest*, and to our Commissary in the City of *Amsterdam*, *Sieur Romswinkel*, at our Charge, to furnish all those of the said Religion (who shall address themselves unto them) with what Vessels and Provisions they shall stand in need of, for the Transportation of themselves, their Goods and Families, from *Holland* to the City of *Hamburg* : Where then our Councellor and Resident for the Circle of the Lower *Saxony*, *Sieur Guerick*, shall furnish them with all Conveniencies they may stand in need of, to convey them further, to whatsoever City or Province they shall think fit to pitch upon, for the Place of their Abode.

### I I.

Those who shall come from the Parts of *France* about *Sedan*, as from *Champagne*, *Lorain*, *Burgundy*, or from any of the *Southern* Provinces of that Kingdom, and who think it not convenient to pass through *Holland*, may betake themselves to the City of *Frankfort* upon *Maine* ; and there address themselves to *Sieur Merain*, our Councellor and Agent in the said City, or in the City of *Cologne* to *Sieur Lely*, our Agent, to whom We have also given Command to furnish them with Money, Passports, and Boats, in order to the carrying them down the River *Rhine*, to our Dutchy of *Cleves* and *Mark* : or in case they shall desire to go further up in our Dominions, our said Ministers and Officers shall furnish them with Address, and Conveniencies, for to Arrive at those several respective Places.

### I I I.

And forasmuch as the said our Provinces are stored with all sorts of Conveniencies, and Commodities, not only for the necessity of Living, but also for Manufactures, Commerce, and Trade by Sea, and by Land; those who are willing to Settle themselves in any of our said Provinces, may choose such Place, as they please, in the Country of *Cleve*, *Mark*, *Ravensberg* and *Minde*, or in those of. *Magdeburg*, *Halberstadt*, *Brandenburg*, *Pomerania*, and *Prussia*. And forasmuch as We conceive, that in our Electoral *Marquisate*, the Cities of *Stendel*, *Werbe*, *Rathenow*, *Brandenburg*, and *Frankfort* ; and in the Country of *Magdeburg*, the Cities

Cities of *Magdenburg, Halle*, and *Calbe* ; and in *Prussia,* the City of *Konigsberg* will be moft commodious, as well for the great abundance of all Neceffaries of Life, which may be had there at cheap Rates, as for the Conveáience of Trade and Traffick ; We have given charge, that as foon as any of the faid *French Proteftants* fhall arrive in any of the faid Cities, they fhall be kindly received and agreed with about all thofe Things, which fhall be thought needful for their Settlement. And for the reft, leaving them at their full Liberty to difpofe of themfelves in whatfoever City or Province they fhall judge moft commodious, and beft fuiting with their Occafions.

### I V.

All the Goods, Houfhold-ftuff, Merchandize, and Commodities, which they fhall bring along with them, fhall not be liable to any Cuftom or Impoft ; but fhall be wholly exempt from all Charges and Impofitions, of what Name or Nature foever they may be.

### V.

And in cafe that in any of the Cities, Towns, or Villages, where the faid Perfons of the *Reformed Religion* do intend to Settle themfelves, there be found any Ruinous and decay'd Houfes, or fuch as ftand empty, and which the Proprietors are not in a condition to Repair, We will caufe the fame to be Affigned to them, the faid *French Proteftants*, as their Propriety, and to their Heirs forever ; and fhall content the prefent Proprietors, according to the Value of the faid Houfes ; and fhall wholly free the fame from all Charges, to which the fame might ftand engaged, whether by Mortgage, Debts, or any other way whatfoever. Furthermore, Our Will is, That they be furnifhed with Timber, Quick Lime, Stones, Bricks, and other Materials they may ftand in need of, for the Repairing of whatfoever is decay'd or Ruinous in any of the faid Houfes ; which fhall, for Six Years, be exempt from all forts of Impofitions, Free-Quarter, and all other Charges whatfoever : Neither fhall the faid *French*, during the faid time of Six Years, be lyable to any Payments whatfoever, but what are chargeable upon things of daily Confumption.

### V I.

In Cities or elfewhere, where convenient Places fhall be found for to build Houfes, thofe of the *Reformed Religion*, who fhall make

their

their Retreat into Our Dominions, fhall be fully Authorized and Im-powered to take Poffeffion of the fame, for themfelves and their Heirs after them, together with all the Gardens, Fields, and Pafture-Grounds belonging to the fame, without being oblig'd to pay any of the dues and charges, with which the faid places, or their dependances may be Incumbred. Moreover, for the facilitating their Building in any of the faid places, We will caufe them to be furnifhed with all the materials they fhall ftand in need of; and will over and above al-low them Ten Years of Exemption, during which they fhall not be lyable to any other charges or payments, befides the dues charged upon things of daily fpending. And furthermore, forafmuch as Our intent is, to make their Settlement in Our Dominions the moft eafie and commodious for them that may be; We have given Command to Our Magiftrates and other Officers in the faid Provinces, to make enquiry, in every City, for Houfes that are to be Lett, into which it fhall be free for the faid *French* to enter, and take up their Lodging as foon as they fhall Arrive; and do promife to pay for them and their Families for Four Years, the Rent of the faid Houfes, provided that they engage themfelves, within the faid Term, to Build in fuch pla-ces as fhall be Affigned to them, in manner, and upon condition as aforefaid.

## VII.

As foon as they fhall have taken up their Habitation in any City or Town of Our Dominions, they fhall immediately be made Free of the place, as alfo of that particular Corporation, which by their Trade or Profeffion they belong to; and fhall enjoy the felf-fame Rights and Priviledges, which the Citizens, Burgeffes, and Freemen of the faid places or Corporations do enjoy, and that without being obliged to pay any thing for the faid Freedome, and without being lyable to the Law of Efcheatage, or any other of what Nature foever they may be, which in other Countries are in force againft Strangers; but fhall be look'd upon, and Treated upon all accounts, in the fame manner, as Our own Natural Subjects.

## VIII.

All thofe whofe are willing to undertake and Eftablifh any Manu-factures; whether of Cloth, Stuffs, Hats, or any other whatfoever, fhall not only be furnifhed with all the Priviledges, Patents, and Franchifes, which they can wifh for, or defire; but moreover We will

take

take care that they be aſſiſted with Moneys, and ſuch other Proviſions and Neceſſaries as ſhall be thought fit to promote and make their undertaking ſucceſsful.

## IX.

To Country-men and others, who are willing to Settle themſelves in the Countrey, We will cauſe a certain extent of Ground to be allotted for them to Till and Cultivate, and give Orders for their being aſſiſted and furniſhed with all things neceſſary for their Subſiſtence, at the beginning of their Settlement; in like manner as we have done to a conſiderable number of *Swiſs*-Families, who are come to dwell in Our Dominions.

## X.

And as for any buſineſs of Law, or matter of difference which may ariſe amongſt thoſe of the *Reformed Religion*, We do grant and allow that in thoſe Cities where any conſiderable number of *French*-Families ſhall be Settled, they be Authorized to chooſe one from amongſt themſelves, who ſhall have full power to decide the ſaid differences in a friendly way, without any formality of Law whatſoever: And in caſe any Differences ſhall ariſe between the *Germans* and the ſaid *French*, that then the ſaid Differences ſhall be decided joyntly by the Magiſtrate of the Place, and by the Perſon whom the *French* ſhall have Choſen for that purpoſe, from amongſt themſelves. And the ſame ſhall be done when the Differences of *Frenchmen*, amongſt themſelves, cannot be accommodated in the forementioned friendly way, by the Perſon thereto by them Elected.

## XI.

In every City, where any numbers of *French* ſhall Settle themſelves, We will maintain a Miniſter, and appoint a convenient place for the Publick Exerciſe of Religion in the *French* Tongue, according to the Cuſtome, and with the ſame Ceremonies which are in uſe amongſt the *Reformed* in *France*.

## XII.

And foraſmuch as ſuch of the Nobility of *France*, who, heretofore, have put themſelves under Our Protection, and entred into our Service, do actually enjoy the ſame Honours, Dignities, and Immunities with thoſe of the Countrey; and that there are many found amongſt them, who have been raiſed to the chief Places and Charges of Our Court, and Command over Our Forces; We are ready and willing to continue the ſame Favour to thoſe of the ſaid Nobility, who for time

to

to come fhall Settle themfelves in our Dominions, by beftowing upon them the feveral Charges, Honours and Dignities, they fhall be
found fitted for. And in cafe they fhall purchafe any Mannors or
Lordfhips, they fhall poffefs the fame with all the Rights, Prerogatives,
and Immunities, which the Nobility of our own Dominions do of
Right enjoy.

## XIII.

All thefe Priviledges and Advantages forementioned fhall not only
be extended to thofe *French* of the *Reformed Religion*, who fhall Arrive in our Dominions (in order to their Settling there) after the
Date of this Declaration; but alfo to thofe, who before the date hereof, have Settled themfelves in our Countries, provided they have been
forced to leave *France* upon account of their Religion; they of the
*Romifh* Profeffion being wholly excluded from any part or fhare therein.

## XIV.

In every one of Our Provinces, Dutchies, and Principalities, We
fhall appoint and Eftablifh certain Commiffioners, to whom the *French*
of the *Reformed Religion*, may have Recourfe, and Addrefs themfelves
upon all occafions of need; and this not only at the beginning of their
Settlement, but alfo afterwards. And all Governours and Magiftrates of Our Provinces and Territories, fhall have order by Vertue
of thefe Prefents, as well as by other particular Commands, We fhall
from time to time Iffue forth, to take the faid Perfons of the *Reformed
Religion* into their Protection, and to maintain them in all the Priviledges here before mentioned, and not fuffer the leaft hurt or injury
to be done unto them, but rather all manner of Favour, Aide and
Affiftance.


*Given at* Poftdam,
Octob. 26. 1685.

# Signed,

## *Frederick William.*

### *Kind*

*Kind Reader,*

FOrafmuch as in the Edict of the *French* King, the perpetual and irrevocable Edict of *Nantes* is recall'd and abolifhed ; I thought fit (becaufe the whole Edict would be too long to be Inferted here) to give you fome paffages of the Prefatory part of it, whereby it may appear what ftrefs was laid on it by *Henry* the IV. (called the Great) Grandfather to the prefent *French* King, and how much he judged the exact maintaining of it would conduce to the Settlement, Peace, and Profperity of his Kingdom.

———*Now it hath pleafed God to give us a beginning of enjoying fome Reft, we think, we cannot employ our felves better, than to apply to that which may tend to the Service and Glory of his Holy Name, and to provide that He may be Adored and Prayed to by all Our Subjects ; and if it hath not yet pleafed him to permit it to be in one and the fame Form of Religion, that it may at the leaft be with one and the fame Intention, and with fuch Rules, that may prevent amongft them all Troubles and Tumults ; and that We and this Kingdom may always conferve the Glorious Title of* Moft Chriftian, *and by the fame means take away the Caufe of Mifchief and Trouble, which may happen from the actions of Religion, which of all others are moft prevalent and penetrating. For this caufe, acknowledging this affair to be of the greateft Importance, and worthy of the beft confideration, after having confidered the Complaints of Our Catholick Subjects, and having alfo permitted to Our Subjects of the* Reformed Religion, *to affemble themfelves by Deputies for framing their Complaints, and making a Collection*

*lection of all their Remonstrances, and having thereup-*
*on conferred divers times with them, we have upon the*
*whole judged it necessary, to give to all Our said Sub-*
*jects one General Law, clear, plain, and absolute, by*
*which they shall be regulated in all differences, which*
*have heretofore risen among them, or which may rise*
*hereafter, and wherewith both the one and the other may*
*be contented; having had no other regard in this deli-*
*beration, than solely the Zeal we have to the Service*
*of God, praying that He would henceforward grant to all*
*Our Subjects a Durable and Established Peace: And*
*We implore and expect from his Divine Bounty the same*
*Protection and Favour he hath always bestowed upon*
*this Kingdom from our Birth, & that He would give our*
*said Subjects the Grace to understand, that in observati-*
*on of this Our Ordinance, consisteth (next to their Duty*
*towards God and us) the principal Foundation of their*
*Union, Concord, Tranquility, Rest, & the re-establishment*
*of this Estate in its first Splendor, Opulency & Strength;*
*as on our part We promise that all the parts of it shall be*
*exactly observed, without suffering any contravention.*
*And for these causes, having with the Advice of the*
*Princes of Our Blood, other Princes and Officers of Our*
*Crown, and other great and eminent Persons of our Coun-*
*cil of State, well and diligently weighed and considered*
*all this Affair; We have by this Edict or Statute, perpe-*
*tual and Irrevocable, Said, Declared, & Ordained, &c.*

F I N I S.